WINTER CROSSINGS

Other books by the author

Poetry

Schooled For Life
Getting On: Poems 2000–2012
Haiku At Seventy
Haiku Of Five Decades
Unholy Empires
Judging By Disappearances
Skeleton Keys
Selected Poems 1956–96
Omnibus Occasions
Beautiful Is Enough
Living Jazz
Safe Levels
Cat Kin
Out Of Exile
Milesian Fables
Robe Of Skin

Fiction

Nine novels including
The Summer Ghosts
Strange Alphabet
The Drive North, etc

Non-Fiction

Jean Rhys revisited
Jean Rhys Afterwords

Translations

Maldoror & Complete Works (Lautréamont)
Days And Nights (Jarry)
Flesh Unlimited: Three Novels (Apollinaire & Aragon)
Masochism In America (MacOrlan)
Surrealist Games (Breton, Eluard, etc*)*
Heliogabalus (Artaud)
The Nun (Péret)

WINTER CROSSINGS

POEMS 2012–2020

ALEXIS LYKIARD

All rights reserved. No part of this work covered by the copyright herein may be reproduced or used in any means—graphic, electronic, or mechanical, including copying, recording, taping, or information storage and retrieval systems—without written permission of the publisher.

Printed by imprintdigital
Upton Pyne, Exeter
www.digital.imprint.co.uk

Typesetting and cover design by narrator
www.narrator.me.uk
info@narrator.me.uk
033 022 300 39

Published by Shoestring Press
19 Devonshire Avenue, Beeston, Nottingham, NG9 1BS
(0115) 925 1827
www.shoestringpress.co.uk

First published 2020
© Copyright: Alexis Lykiard
© Cover image: Mario Caruso on Unsplash

The moral right of the author has been asserted.

ISBN 978-1-912524-62-4

ACKNOWLEDGEMENTS

Thanks to the writer friends, magazine editors and colleagues—Kevin Bailey, Ken Clay, Alan Dent, Tony Roberts and Tony Simpson—in whose publications many of these poems first appeared, sometimes in very different versions: *Acumen*, *Chapman*, *Crazy Oik*, *Frogmore Papers*, *HQ* (*Haiku Quarterly*), *MQB* (*Mistress Quickly's Bed*), Penniless Press, *Poetry In The Blood* (Shoestring Press, 2014) and *The Spokesman*.

My special thanks to John Lucas, author-publisher extraordinaire, for his continued advice and enthusiasm.

THEATRE

(for MFL)

Meeting in middle age when life had scarred
Us both, might speed appreciation of the good
In others, the best in ourselves, and thus it proved.
The rest of life, the better half, that lay ahead
Would hold joy and fulfilment too long missed:
We seemed like lucky players time blessed, fortune kissed.
Thirty years spent close together—these have been

Filled with abiding happiness and pleasures, few hard
Times. Love brought surprises, furthered our delight.
Whatever days remain, the only certain
Thing, while any wounds of age throb unforeseen,
Is that we lived life to the full, loved and were loved,
And knew how sun warms and restores. Soon unknown night
Will bring an end, ring down the velvet curtain.

CONTENTS

Winter Crossing	1
Birth Days	2
Incubus	3
A Filial Piece	4
Eyes Off The Doomsday Clock	5
Transitional	6
Shaken	8
Wiseing Up, Winding Down	9
"When You Are Old…"	11
Writers And Their Works	12
My Rhymer's CV	13
A Changing City Garden	14
Colour Charts	15
At 77	16
Oldgoatsong	17
Taking Lines For A Walk	18
Moore's Apples	19
The Appetite For Words	20
Ends And Meanings	22
N F T	23
Ballad Of B-Movies	24
Glum Thoughts, Listening To Verdi's *Requiem*	25
De Mortuis Nil Nisi Bonum	26
The Late Reading	27
Threnody	28
Bataille Du *Moi*	29
Finishing Up	30
Everyone Their Island	31
Like	35
Labouring The Point—A Colonial Question	36
Cold Comfort, Finally	37
Mind The Gap!	38
Home Improvement At A Price	39
Goethedämmerung	40
Views From A Third-Floor Balcony	42
Song Of Senex The Cynic	43

Foolhardy Perennials	44
The Old Sleep Less	45
Survival Kit	46
BPPV	47
Nocturne	48
Net Result	49
Cold Season	50
Notes	52

WINTER CROSSING

St Malo–Plymouth 2013

This ferry trip from France takes far too long—ordeal indeed.
For fear of following through, I dare not fart:
my saturnine and sceptic nature means that Art
cannot console on such occasions, where maybe it should.
Distraction's useless, prayers to non-existent gods no good;
pills and wrist-bands don't help. What price an efficacious trick
to help dispel the gut-ache and stave off being sick?
I'd cast away the book I feel too ill to read

for some dry crumb of comfort I could share
with wretched and still-worse-afflicted you…
Its author's trisyllabic surname nearly sinks from view.
(The French, as linguists note, pronounce it more like two
slow, beautiful, delirious beats.) While angling for a rhyme
to divert mid-November nausea, in the nick of time
I focus on Nadar's grim photograph of Baudelaire,
and manage to avoid *Les Fleurs Du Mal de mer*.

BIRTH DAYS

After a long engagement, there were seven years
or so of marriage. Then my parents managed
to get me—an outcome seen as rather late
amid the affluent Athenian circles
during those tensely charged and vexing Thirties.
I was their only child, belated son
whose agonising birth, after her own long wait,
must have been traumatic, if not burdensome
enough to test even the fittest woman at that time.
I happened to be overdue, weighed heavy, a breech birth,
as if reluctant to emerge, breathe troubled air

Beginning life too quick upon the start
of World War Two. Today though, I can only guess
what she went through, having survived in infancy
a bout of meningitis several years before
the First World War. She who was never physically strong
would die aged fifty-three. Contrast
my father, who self-righteously could moan about
his being 'not long for this world', and yet was one
well able to survive into his nineties.
Mother's fatal set of complications meant
her short life finished helplessly, in coma

Ending that seemed unbearable, prompting regret
since I was told too late, too far away to travel back
from France in time to bid farewell to her
before both consciousness and life were lost.
Sorrows live on, reflected within passing years;
perhaps these days they're fitting, these few birthday thoughts:
seventy-seven's the house number, my new age.
It's fitting also that my ageing body's
hernia should be umbilical… Sometime soon
we shall again be one, both worlds conjoined, reborn
as whirling atoms, dancing particles of dust.

INCUBUS

These days if I stare into mirrors I grow
vexed with myself almost—scared I'm resembling
that bitter-spirited old man my father.
It seems hard to avoid such an uncanny likeness,
although I try not to adopt those Charles Boyer
suave frowns, or (low angle shot) the Mussolini
glare, dapper yet stern. Called in youth a clumsy dunce,

I've aged, wary of cold deceits: at least I know
now I'm still Me, was never that hateful Other…
Opting for truth not vanity, I more than once
glimpsed a sharp, unsettling insight without any
clear sense of either life or work as perfect flow.
Dissembling's done with, but there's no flight in this case
from one's own ghost, and what's been termed *the family face*.

A FILIAL PIECE

He always would complain he'd had things hard.
Self-preservation, if not true necessity,
was why he was best pleased to wash his hands of me.
He guessed I'd learn his story, hence the curse
on me... Mine's a partial view of my father,
of course, who feared exposure and therefore
wasted his life rewriting history.
In time we must accept the past. Far rather
call it quits: it isn't worth being bitter,
dwelling on lies. Instead one tries to escape from more
typecasting, careful not to end up worse
off, just his understudy, a sad kind of bastard.

EYES OFF THE DOOMSDAY CLOCK

Ageing, you're very aware of every threat to existence—
More than ever the evident frailties of friend or acquaintance
Alike—while what will be coyly labelled fatalities
Proliferate, are numbered with quick or sorry obsequies.

Oblivious we remain, and shun mainly grim news unceasing,
Increasing our ostrich mode. The noisome political scum
Come readily rising to the top, bent on subjugating all,
Falling only belatedly, well after their damage is done.

None now is cheerful unduly, since whatever power
Our petty worlds can still wield, wild bigots and despots exercise:
Lies abound for general use. As Vonnegut wrote, *So It Goes…*
Suppose then all warmongers crazy, for they almost always are,
Far removed from reason or truth. Life on yet another fading star
's arbitrary, spins to dust. Through greed and neglect this planet dies.

TRANSITIONAL

1

It might be tempting fate to seek to fill the brain's
far narrower, if not yet empty, chambers:
septuagenarian veins remain however warm;
dreams pulse with fresher-seeming blood from distant times.

Here's the last sight of sun as it declines
and glistens at the margin of recall
beyond all reason. This brings momentary pain
as, almost imperceptible from the Aegean dusk,
cicadas sing once more, susurrant. There's no need
to strain to listen, dreamers summon them again
with ease, since every shadowed past contains some such
recurrent souvenir, echoes that tease and fade too soon.

The movie next turns monochrome, becomes a loop
of bleached, stark contrasts, long white beaches, blackened
rock pools, haunts where one swam with lovers naked,
and secret grottoes under cliffs: you could keep cool,
relishing the welcome shade, a respite and relief
from life's grey list of aches and each banal regret.
But still nostalgia stalks those younger passions burnt away
in stifling rooms or fiercest blaze of island noon…

2

Meals with muses at midday, ouzo, loaves of bread
and olives, bodies linked beneath the pines in steep
places where goats liked best to clamber, browsing
green-shaded slopes; theirs were the faintest, brightest sounds
to draw a drowsy couple out of sleep. After the bells
came louder, scrambling hooves, dislodging the dry soil
and lukewarm stones during the hunt for a securer track,
easier footholds, surer paths, succulent herbs to munch.
They knew the highest places which we loved so much,

those zones of hidden pleasures: there each exile goes,
while lovers kid themselves that time will not run out
and moments of euphoria and joy may last
without the subtle echo of a summer lost.
Perhaps we overstayed, for always it proved hard to leave
when each day melted happily away, until
persistent scents of thyme and resin dwindled in the dark,
gave way on our nocturnal strolls to waves of jasmine,
the night flowers drinking starshine all around the bay…

3

We'd lie relaxed after a swim, and as salt dried
like sperm across her gleaming limbs, so it all seemed
a happy, natural form of encrustation,
a sort of spectral portent of some life to come,
breeding the memories that might endure
and haunt us for as long as fanciful
imagination beckoned. How one flicks through these
old keepsakes of hours fugitive, lived lovingly

and cherished! Odd though, when on calm, near-perfect days,
a yearning still persisted for landscapes of home;
the focus sharpened to expose returning dread,
fear of return, of new routines that lay in wait,
responsibility assumed, angst unavoidable.
A dreary chorus would commence (CASH & CAREER)
to vitiate both physical and mental
voyages, or sour the taste of youth's fine wine…

Late in the day I try to gather and reflect
on reminiscences of all too many years
ago; they prove elusive, difficult to find
or recollect, except by stubborn stumbling toward art.
How else to clear the cluttered fragments of an aging mind,
regain the purer, barer islands of the heart?

SHAKEN

'The earth last moved for me in 1979'.
(An opening line perhaps, to play for laughs or sympathy?)
Panic-stricken, we forsook a friendly *kafkenéion*—
Dashed out as walls cracked and some plaster fragments fell.
The silent beach was only yards away, the lukewarm sea
Seemed calm enough that night, the usual stars ashine,
With bright foam gleaming on the wave-crests, plus a hint of swell

And that was all, almost an anti-climax. On
The remotest shore of southern Samos once again,
In one's own seventies sleep, this traveller feels no pain,
No urgent joy, nor any qualms at ancient history.
Tremors from the unsettling past are soundless though, no sign
Of firmer ground ahead.... But is it tinnitus, that bell
Deep in the brain, an obligato to odd dreams of mine?

WISEING UP, WINDING DOWN

(Triptych for three Graces)

1 Verbal

(D.G.L.)

One winter morning long ago, I travelled
with a lover to the Castle. No one else
was there except for a custodian of sorts,
elderly, bespectacled and whiskey-pissed.
He clutched us in turn at the hips as we lay flat
upon our backs: supplicant posture, that. Above
us swam some low, bedraggled clouds. Almost as dank
and grey, the stone block bridged a gap in the tower's
top edge. The Sixties ending, curious time... Yet good
to be young, involved in wild escapes, till lawyers'
lingo seemed a grim pantomime few understood.
How to acquire their sober, glibly fluent tongue?
Wishful, we both hung back, stared up at the cold slab.
Impassive Gaelic masonry. Gift of the gab
it promised, though: the Blarney Stone got fondly kissed.

2 Umbilical

(K.J.D.)

The Nineties: my own fifties, a good time ago,
with my new wife discovering our newer life
and sharing many gifts of fortune—these unsought
if striven for. We navigated darker streams
of legal nonsense, access, custody and courts,
to find ourselves (the cliché apt if imprecise)
'in a special place'... This last phrase simply meant
remembering a long-lost land, a sunlit site

of oracles and tripods, laurel leaves, incense
burning, omens, cryptic messages to come

scribbled upon an unbelievably blue sky
over the Omphalos, the navel of the ancient
world. Thus on that hollowed stone I set one thumb,
then made a wish, although not in my mother tongue,
and asked a question which required no answer.
It was enough, at Delphi, to sense deep content.

3 Biblical

   (M.F.L.)

A post-Millennial noon. Greek priest let down the metal pail,
cranking it back with slow, deliberate turns to greet
politely these half-dozen Western travellers—
a mild, sceptical bunch, no pilgrims, but all linked
by growing disbelief and shared distaste for politics.
Weighing up myths, we marvelled that a Christian church
could suavely welcome walkers, boast of renovation
on a lavish scale while, so close by at Nablus,
a myriad refugees crammed into the Balata camp.

A mortal right's too often claimed; the strict religionist
may terrorize and kill, evict and dispossess the natives:
such seems the fate of Palestine—the Promised Land, say thieves,
those Zionists and zealous settlers who impose
their own apartheid on the mainly Muslim *Untermensch*.
What deity exists, empowered to promise anything?
Context is all, not blinkered folly; purer vision's missed,
as are new angles. One might wish for some cool insight gained
through thinking clear and drinking deep from Jacob's Well.

"WHEN YOU ARE OLD…"

That variation Yeats once wrote
On Ronsard's sonnet, which I read
So long ago at boarding school,
Made youthfully romantic sense…
I'm nodding by the open fire,
The past seems dead, a half-closed book,
Not worth a second look. You led

An anxious life, yearned to fly higher,
Escape harsh rules, cold baths, the Bell,
Nonsense from bullies, daily dread…
A writer's life meant living well,
The best revenge of innocents.
No fool, it's said, like an old fool:
You burned your boats yet kept afloat.

WRITERS AND THEIR WORKS

A motley crowd, crammed elements on dusty shelves,
Names and fast-fading shadows of our mortal selves,
Although some restless, more insistent ghost may walk

Or rather drift, among *Collected Works* and *Table-Talk,*
Scandals, biographies of *So-and-So, The Poems of Y.*
Words, like written lives, are ranked, wondrous or plainly rotten;
Whether they truth-told, entertained, or sold an abject lie,

Books to treasure remain few, their origins forgotten.
Judgements are rarely final, literary or otherwise—
Only one certainty abides: the author dies.

MY RHYMER'S CV

Forced plant, if often awkward learner. Early tried
the fine weight of new worlds of language, to extract
some hardwon certainties from ash. Strove not to hide
hurt deeper than burnt fingers. While dissatisfied,
found 'proper jobs'—all too prosaic; got sidetracked.
Poetry (its elusive truth) can't be denied.

A CHANGING CITY GARDEN

¿Le Gusta Este Jardín? ... ¡Evite Que Sus Hijos Lo Destruyan!

An ancient bath, whose metal feet once clawed
at fitted carpet, perched on slabs of stone:
my artist friend painted its flanks a skyblue matt.
It turned into an earth-filled plant-vase, iron throne,
enamelled relic of the Forties house
you well recalled; so now we could accord
it pride of place... In latter days, the tall bamboos

Sprouted where previously an outside privy stood;
still later, roses rambled for all to enjoy.
That leafy jungle's vanished, as has our old cat,
the venerable Claude, who there in comfort sat,
jeered at by squirrels, too slow to catch bird or mouse.
No cause to move though—best improve, but not destroy
our *rus in urbe*—this last choice proved good.

COLOUR CHARTS

Here's one unanswerable question: what is Blue?
Invisibility becoming wholly visible,
always transparently my own—retorts the shade of Klein;
opting for the abyss, to test the sky's true emptiness
he placed due emphasis on style, ambiguous utterance.
Space without borders should reflect sublimity…The fine
Idea spread to dissolve romantic precepts, muddle, mess,

those sad, blurred mirrors of ourselves… *Ultramarine*?
An impure mixture, not a global trademark-hue!
But Malcolm Lowry did distill more lurid brews
and reinvented Siren-songs long-faded, though he knew
voluble minds might founder on a tide of blues.
Nostalgia dominant blots out coherence,
with art drowned in a silence incorruptibly sea-green.

AT 77

A heavy package, half-inch thick, thuds on the front-door mat.
It's March, the finely-printed College Yearbook's here,
Chronicling Honours, Fellowships, distinctions of all sorts,
And arcane titles dear to academics, plus the top degrees.
Provost's Report—Professor Somebody's, whose name is new
    to me;
I clock how young he looks, compared to me at least;
Strange also, to recall my undergraduate days,
And skim these full, most fulsome, celebratory Obits

Of various contemporaries. A vague curiosity, if that,
Seeps in as I review the faded, dreamlike details,
Fragments of fugitive events, or faces rarely seen again
After the bright intensity of those three, close-packed years.
Herewith some names, DOB, RIP… Nostalgia never fails:
Time to forget steroids and statins, raise a glass to mutter *Cheers!*

OLDGOATSONG

During thirty years together
(familiar words aren't wrong)
'old love' survived cold weather,
new struggle left us strong.

Heartfelt rhymes have their own good reason,
home truths help us along,
as when from darkest season
springs deep and honest song.

TAKING LINES FOR A WALK

'A dread of the sonnet', Edward Thomas said he had,
since 'many of the best' seemed 'rhetoric only'.
He detested the workhorse life of the prose-hack,
words forced out of depression, most routinely.

The successful sonneteer might choose to be
'tremendous poet' and/or 'cold mathematician'
with a mind well-disciplined. So how could *he*
'accommodate his thoughts to such a condition'?

Wordsworth, another great walker, managed it,
as did Shakespeare, Donne, John Milton and John Keats.
They hid their mastery, mysterious holy writ
where skill and feeling meet: thus literature's elites

move briskly with an easy stride… Then, via Frost,
Thomas mapped his route, the life that's won, not lost.

MOORE'S APPLES

i.m. Merrill Moore MD (1903–57)

A sonnet a day keeps the doctor away.
An ample store of words will feed the memory,
therefore between hard stints as psychoanalyst
he harvested a myriad calm, uncluttered lines—
grist also to the practice mill, a subtle means
of circumventing daily pressure. What relief,
wry formulae for peace worked out through patience,
a way past all the formless traumas which persist…

How, though, extract a valid style from the despair
of others? Always the puzzling mind, aware
no certainties exist, runs on still noting awkward hints
at what's concealed. To explicate some blurred belief
meant honing one's own meanings, while the neater codes
held healing truths as well as wild, audacious odes.

THE APPETITE FOR WORDS

All of the menu *Special*, though of course 'You can't
go home again'. Things change, reveal they aren't
quite what one thought them. Places rarely were
mere food for our convenience… I prefer
to savour out-to-lunch inventions that delight me,
banquets of words, GREECE SPECIALITY.

I still recall how, long ago in Camden Town,
a Greek greengrocer could displace my frown,
through some Hellenic coinage I thought fine.
One such dispelled dull care—his GREYFRUIT sign…
Now, the pure poetic spirit that coheres
in Crete's tavernas entertains and cheers.

Words happily increase the hunger, so we find;
the senses reel as wonder fills the mind.
GIRO IN PLATE. LAMP HEADS.
SOSITJES. GRETAN HOT PIE.
STAFFED PIPER. STUFF TOMATOE.
DONAT. CRUASSAN.

Travellers can slake their thirst: MILK SAKE
is crossed out, and renamed MILK SHEIK,
while disputatious feminists may choose
MANHATIN COCKTOIL to chase off their blues.
SILECT APPERTIVES also, like JIN-FIZZ,
suggest that multifarious drinking is

on offer. Leaving this auspicious place
we'll very likely never see again,
I catch her eye. She seems almost in pain,
suppressing laughter, hand up to flushed face,
viewing some purely practical advice…
It's a vital fact of life, no mere hortative caper,
that sign scrawled on the wall above the WC,

whose words, chalked with polite universality,
are what she seeks to indicate to me.
A cheerful note to leave on, in contented vein!
So off we go, following poetry and logic's flow,
glad to obey the rules, without throwing in the towel:
    —PLEAS NOT PUT PAPER
    IN THE BOWEL—

ENDS AND MEANINGS

God must be dead: the dreaded despot in the sky,
(if there's a 'He' at all) omnipotently fair,
devised a heavy game-plan, those light years ago,
for one small globe—strange fancy gone awry.
Man maketh Myth and War, so who's to tell or know

whose head shall roll, stay wholly covered, and whose hair
may be short-cropped or sprout, which way to grow?
Playthings of Fate, and our own dupes, how should we go
about a life that's brief, based on some fluent lie?
Religion sells us short: ours not to reason *Why*.

N F T

Some of my happiest London nights and days
were spent exploring Film there, with like-minded friends
during the Sixties. But every youthful decade ends,
dismissed or analysed as just another transient phase
we're cured of, when more sober adults. Now I know
these three initials that describe the passing show

Here in our deepest, culturally-deprived South-West,
stand for a different sort of mental interest.
This code often appears in local doctors' notes,
a useful form of shorthand: no need for long quotes
or doubtful clinical assessments rambling on and on,
when such a patient simply is **N**(ormal) **F**(or) **T**(iverton).

BALLAD OF B-MOVIES

Old celluloid awakens nightmare—
limousine speed beyond control
or else you're drowning in a quagmire
where monsters may devour you whole.

The parachute that will not open.
The slowly unlocked, creaking door.
You're certain those loud footsteps quicken
to match your walk, quite as before.

And zombies lumber down the hallway,
clumsily shuffle… Funny, though,
that none outpace the creeping panic:
to hide is useless, as you know.

Stuck in a lift, the button jammed. It's
thirty flights up. Now do you dare
to clamber into total darkness
or scream for help, when no one's there?

A vampire flaps at gaping window,
silk cape bloodshot as his eyes.
Flash of fangs laid bare to bite you
but you can't stir, numb with surprise.

Rush through the graveyard—shapes are moving
shrouded in grey between the tombs.
What floats nearby is nothing human:
ahead of you some creature looms.

It's tried and tested—laugh at horror,
then pinch yourself until you wake…
Which always works. Except for this time
when voices whisper *No mistake*.

GLUM THOUGHTS, LISTENING TO VERDI'S *REQUIEM*

How strange and random human life can seem—
So many friends both close and distant fallen ill
Or struggling with poor health. Fragility's advance
Is sure yet often stealthy, sickness soon laid bare;
Meanwhile excisions and extractions, accidents,

Collapse, are words which govern us until
Insomnia itself succumbs to the Last Dream—
The one that means your number's up—the lottery of age
Whose wheel ensures nobody wins, with no chance there
Of cheering outcomes, nor much point to rage.

DE MORTUIS NIL NISI BONUM

[*Kaleidoscope*, BBC Radio 4, 30th December 1981]

As good as Shelley and in some ways even better,
averred the late Australian poet Peter Porter,
quick to drop the old, anarchic macho mask of Oz
and hail the flawed legacy of ill-starred Sylvia Plath.
Why though, award laurels—those illustrious classic bays—
for chaos or bruised, ingrown talents? Critics ought to
ruminate objectively that suicidal days
and early deaths aren't merit badges, while more measured praise
averts absurdity, forestalling Apollonian wrath.

THE LATE READING

i.m. P.R. (1946–2011)
Sunt aliquid manes…

Elegies angst and anger
freighted fully with compassion
Syllabics packed tight with humour

Elements often unwelcome
but artefacts few should ignore
Classical patterns well-weighted
subversive still in their function

No more exasperation, waiting in line by the inky Styx
Birdwatching a thing of the past—though a clear view of
 Charon's craft—
Thus the world-weary poet departs, first downing one farewell
 draught
Fine bardic words not required (libations perhaps, on the ferry?)

Oblivion's obol paid, no obvious mark of deletion
Awaits an obsessive maker, so artful and contrary…
Life's mill grinds on, but he's well away from our mortal politics.

THRENODY

Eheu fugaces, Postume,
Postume, labuntur anni…
Horace's lines on time fleeting
speak truth more distinctly to me.

Eheu fugaces… What of old friends?
The jazz musicians are mostly dead,
yet life's wild harmony never ends:
words and memories whirl through my head…

BATAILLE DU *MOI*

O, what will become of Me
as the brain-cells daily die?
Farewell sex and poetry—
it's the Story Of The I.

FINISHING UP

What niggling irritations of old age!
Grim fates of Nagg and Nell and Beckett tramps
are far from fiction, nearer documentary now.
Each pause and stasis may suggest a smouldering rage;
the candles madly gutter, ancient lamps
burn low, obscuring slowly the smeared page,
which stays unturned and blurred until the bell

of that last sacred cow is heard to toll,
not tinkle... No philosopher, no comic sage
can explicate, dismiss the night, convincingly console,
tell po-faced jokes about brief lives, great books unread.
Despite pains felt or taken, one's a long time dead
for sure, and soon enough the game ends, anyhow.

EVERYONE THEIR ISLAND

'upon the sands of ever-crumbling hours' – Beddoes

Those islands dreamed of once again
so fleetingly possessed by heart and mind,
places and pleasures that you never will revisit…
Is it the memory alone of islands
waking you from uneasy, restless sleep
most recently, after you sailed back across
the lost years, then away toward a mere
three score and ten?—A reverie of Samos,
the dog-days of that summer, 1979,
longing for the conclusion of a sleepless
Aegean night; confined inside a stifling room,
barely a cubicle as I recall, a bright
white cell that overlooked the darkened
harbour and the somewhat squalid, ill-lit quay…

Unable to lie close to one another—
with her so near and yet so far from me—
we both awaited the elusive daylight,
dawn keeping an uneasy distance still,
the pair of us most anxious not to miss
the early morning ferry to Piraeus.
Heading for Athens after months abroad we were
exhausted yet reluctant to return,
nostalgic for an England that we never guessed
during our absence had irrevocably
changed course, and for so very much the worse,
just as our time together would be changing too,
only a further three years left to run…

That desperately tormented sleepless night
remained one to remember, fraught enough, spent
somewhere in a limbo neither could invent
nor later joke about, though both might try.
We had been trapped by pipedreams of escape,

and now were transitory guests constrained
unwillingly by cramped twin beds, on threadbare
greying mattresses, within that narrow room,
inside an uninviting, mercifully temporary
refuge—the brief last-minute haven offered
us grudgingly by the misnamed Hotel
Morpheus. That fitful, wretched sultry night
of feverish insomnia wrote Finis
to a shining, wondrous episode, remote
survival, part of a shared past, our younger days.
Was it simply those mosquitoes I recall?
How could it have stayed too hot for shelter?

Best make the best of things and brave the glare
of that bare central lightbulb blazing to expose
our sunburnt nakedness, our hedonist fragility,
and better thus to see one's foes than not.
But always, diving from the outer dark, that whine,
the drone of all those dreadful inescapable
squadrons, kamikazes of relentless insects…
There was no balm, no remedy except
to doze and start and start to curse and then
to slap oneself and then each other and again
try to drowse or drive them off and stop
their draining of our healthy, over-heated blood.

And so we sweltered, sweated, laughed and swore
in order not to scratch an itch or wince with pain;
frustration set in, fear of bites became a curse
on sleep or love in that anticlimactic room
without nets, window-mesh, repellent spray
or ointment, and none to complain to. (Anyhow,
our rueful farewells had been made—the lonely hut
upon the beach turned into anecdote). We vowed
to take a toll of all those bloody little pests

and their incredible persistence, needling us
near to anger, an annoyance close to frenzy.
Scores of blotches, squashed red blobs, marked the white walls
and stained our skin but then exhaustion got
the better of us and thus we surrendered
or rather, in an ancient word, succumbed, too hot
and finally too tired to fight, relieved
to have survived our journey to the end of night.

The next day did arrive—a sudden dawn,
time for departures. Only later would I ask
myself exactly what had happened to us there:
why the relief, leaving that isle of marvels, home
to Ritsos and Pythagoras? You soon forget
unique experience, fine wines, an earthquake, scenes
with intrusive priests, packs of wild mountain dogs,
the dusty bus whose tyre burst on a corkscrew bend,
those voyeurs, drunken soldiers, many sorts
of factional dispute, fascists and communists,
irrational taverna feuds and stinging insults,
arguments that loomed significant, stray omens
of a strange, unsettling time, when sea and sun
alone could heal our bodies. As for minds,
we learned extremes could never meet, euphoria
cannot be recreated nor repeated and
anguish was to linger, mingled with regret,
while things deemed threatening then, which once disturbed
us, seemed almost farcical in retrospect.

Given the peculiar twists and turns of those
romantic travels with their well-kept secrets,
unknown destinations—the whole epic voyage
most lives embark on and must comprehend—
we soon accept them, prize the joyful wanderings
and odd ordeals alike, encounters not
so brief, love and luck lasting only as long
as they were meant to, or you've made them. If it seems

each melancholy bout will nonetheless persist
(with unseasonably irritating whispers
in daylight as in darkness), fit to overwhelm
stark clarity and the grey weighty baggage of the mind,
such is old age! When haunted by the past,
stung by a twinge of conscience or regret; in dreams
of other times, faces and islands long since left behind,
so many friends and lovers fading in the mist,
appreciate what words remain to you in praise
of all that was and is. The best and worst of days
you've known: why mourn lack of success or misspent
youth? Needless to wither yet into the Single Truth:
the tortuous trail which lies so near and no one can resist.

LIKE

Less of the simile these days—more a philosophy,
Means to measure pauses, by removing punctuation.
Is this quietly-spoken habit a shallow mindless tic,
A rather queasy substitute for simple empathy?
Adolescent angst, or awkward fragment of a question?

In conversation endlessly the casual word is heard
Without compelling urgency, mere gesture, trope or trick.
Short-cuts in patterns of speech confuse but cannot attract,
And candour advises against a bland, box-ticker click
Of network endorsement; still people seek approbation
Via friendliness poorly feigned, both illusive and too quick.

New Worldly style permits misuse of this four-letter word,
Whose feeblest echoes preclude decent communication.
When corrupted meanings persist, art requires truthful fact;
Hesitant vagueness was never what Aristotle taught.
We're urged in *The Poetics* to learn from self-reflection—
His Poet "perceiving likeness" of a highly rigorous sort.

LABOURING THE POINT—A COLONIAL QUESTION

1st August 2019

The endless, questionable anti-Semitism fuss
Is media-stoked to fool the credulous and hoodwink us—
All those presuming to deplore, or even criticise,
The fact that stolen acres are annexed by Israel.

Much of the so-called Promised Land's a living hell
For its original inhabitants the Palestinian folk,
A peaceful people, whom the Zionists coerced to dwell
Under their military rule, apartheid yoke.

The dispossessed and brutalised—here's irony!—are forced
Through daily cruelty to heed that distant Holocaust
For which they're blameless; elsewhere Gentiles must apologise
Sheepishly for European history, *ad infinitum*.

Politicians, flush with cash, close ranks to sneer and fight them—
Dissenters, any conscience-driven humans who resist
The shrillest imprecations of the Zionist.
And yet what Palestinian would accept this unjust fate,
Repressive occupation by a racist State?

COLD COMFORT, FINALLY

The sunset sky is stippled pink on blue,
The sort of scene that should appeal to me and you,
Though these days there's awareness of what's close:
A certain end to pleasure, love or suffering;
Hints of what Henry James dubbed 'the distinguished thing';
The last requests of artists for more air or light;
Deathbed conversions—desperate insurance!—lachrymose
Farewells, et cetera… Life's a black comedy all right,
The likes of Gogol going gaga and religiose,
Maupassant's wretched fate, wrecked body and wild mind.
Does satisfying work suggest fulfilment of a kind?

MIND THE GAP!

An exhortation one should always take to heart
On tube or train, those three small words express the hurt
Felt in-between my teeth, where the stitched gum—
Extraction's aftermath—hints of some pain to come.

A fortnight spent with sorely bruised and swollen jaw
Feeling touch-sensitive, contains still more
Passages of broken sleep, discomfort, pills
To pop and pap to eat, while paracetamol

Spells torpid, grudged abstention from all alcohol.
Only a masochist would welcome such raw thrills…
Albeit slowly, present tension fades into The Past;
Time and a bright young dentist promise sure relief at last.

HOME IMPROVEMENT AT A PRICE

Rubble and builder's bullshit, weeks of stress, delay and dust,
Then noise, ineptitude, intrusion: why live with all that?
Asthma, fatigue and sleeplessness result; an anxious cat
And fewer laughs, less fun. Drained like our savings, we lose
    weight…
Dreams surely dwindle, while one should expect some loss of trust
In sales talk, tradesmen, 'Project Management'. We old folk must,
It seems, welcome the time and space that's left—surviving, just.

GOETHEDÄMMERUNG

Imperious mandarin in coat of verdigris, he sprawls,
Goethe parked upon a tarnished emerald throne.
The Great Man casts his jaded philosophic eye
over the dull succession of expensive cars
now hurtling down the broad and snow-flecked boulevard.
Beyond the grandiose plinth a single yellow crane
aspires to puncture bloated clouds above Vienna.

"And he wasn't even Austrian", our friend recalls,
noting the sole, correctly-spelled graffito we have seen,
scrawled on a builder's board beside the German genius:
Urban Youth Never Sleeps—an obscure boast, or threat perhaps.
Meanwhile by day the fur-clad female burghers
tread gritted *trottoirs* in big boots and hats, well-preserved folk
wrapped smart and smug within their antiseptic city.

Migrants, Muslims, buskers, beggars have been shovelled elsewhere
so there's not a speck of gum, dogshit or litter
freckling immaculate streets, tram-routes, efficient U-Bahn.
Everything's affluent, conformist, *uber*-clean,
the imperial past as icing-sugar. You can buy
Klimt trinkets, keyrings, Mozart chocolate
bonbons, most ingeniously gross confectionery.

Walk by heavy, decorative gates and ornate railings,
overwrought-ironwork… Looking is
free at any rate, and the economy thriving,
what with the great weight of Capital steadily driving
hearts, minds and lives of Viennese today.
Enormous banks, curlicued façades of whitest buildings,
ranks of horse-drawn cabs, Hapsburg palaces restored post-war,

show that the largely Catholic bourgeoisie has triumphed:
whoever else ought revolutions to be for?
During yet another leisurely, unstructured journey,
we found the old Jewish quarter, deserted in the cold,
then passed a synagogue a single well-armed guard patrolled,
as he strolled near his shiny van marked *Polizei*.
A couple of smaller, more pleasing details caught the eye:

plaques to commemorate some lesser literary lights,
the little-read Stifter and Broch, sounding like attorneys
to the majority of tourist types. The city's edge,
all that satiric questioning, appears rather long gone
one must conclude—only the scattered traces that remain
of dangerous artists, riskily creative minds, those Jews…
True, there's the Freudhaus, or a passing mention of Karl Kraus,

and Joseph Roth the 'holy drinker', who preferred Berlin.
By now we've come to wonder who might feel a
frisson of bohemian sex or deathwish, syphilis and Schiele…
Wandering through the city, with the river on our right,
casually retracing steps to more familiar landmarks,
the four of us remark how—even at the smallest crossroads,
each unimportant intersection—firm rules are obeyed;

Austrians all abide by regulations once laid down.
Everything's *in Ordnung*, therefore everyone observes, must
wait and understand, stand ready for the sign, the right time,
safe and sure, the time that shall surely be, both arrival
and departure, brief moment of expectant certainty,
perception fit to free the spirit and unfreeze the limbs,
bringing a quick flash of unarguable reason—
      the diminutive Green Man.

VIEWS FROM A THIRD-FLOOR BALCONY

[*Gärtnerstrasse, Berlin, Summer 2014*]

The things one thought or did, and often dreamed
of celebrating in some form, assume with age
a quite repetitive if not insistent role,
as though the fragments which our faulty memories
record might still reveal some message from the past.

Great works once read and savoured are reread: each page
exacts a different response; what earlier seemed
significant is not so now. That bell will toll,
its sound more resonant on days like these,
when words lose flavour and spill into air at last.

SONG OF SENEX THE CYNIC

Life's for the living
though each day we're dying,
cold fate unforgiving
for there's no denying

we're in or we're out—
whisper or shout,
turn, turn about—
why are we waiting?

Scheming, creating,
warring and mating,
loving or hating:
the time that's to spend
has only one end.

FOOLHARDY PERENNIALS

Has he read all *those books?* A self-styled dullard asked my wife,
Who was not especially pleased, but felt bound to explain
How the writing of books had always been my life,
And that in learning to write well, writers take time to read.
One's books were like most necessary milestones in a life,
And seemed to choose their owner, marking paths to lead.
No doubt this ever-doubtful question will be asked again.

THE OLD SLEEP LESS

Une nuit, c'est un chemin tournant qu'il faut parcourir de bout en bout
(Drieu la Rochelle, *Le Feu Follet*, 1931)

Flail through all those so-called small hours wide awake:
It seems appalling when there's no effective course to take
Except to court monotony, dull wordgames, lists of stuff,
Ruses to muffle or annul the over-active mind.
And still the would-be sleeper's rarely tired enough
To slip free from the consciousness of Self, beat time's slow grind.

Insomnia suggests each flight is blocked; pills never make
For consolation, nor give grace to set the past behind.
The present warns of future desperation, hour on hour,
Till night turns to belated, longed-for chill of dawn—
The broken day that hints at brightness soon reborn,
With life itself amply restored, brought into flower.

SURVIVAL KIT

Armed with *preventer*, *enabler* and *spacer*,
a backpack of tissues, spectacles, notebook,
bottle of water, you're able to face a
stranger new world. Age with its many changes of outlook
has us question past values—the time ahead shorter,
if full of surprises. When challenged by asthma,
don't surrender to panic, simply move rather slower,
for reason requires that you treasure each breath:
Life's joys become measureless rhyming with Death.

BPPV

Benign Paroxysmal Positional
Vertigo was your young doctor's diagnosis.
Certain maladies may prove less grim than one supposes;
most folk stoically accept 'Age is no bed of roses',
yet any competent physician'll
check, double-check, manipulate and reassure…
We're both relieved, though what each medic knows is
all lives are short or fraught enough, until that final cure.

NOCTURNE

Earworms and distant echoes plague the old
who strain to summon half-remembered rhymes
and fear unwonted heat yet dread the cold.
They're teased by trivial facts from former times,
ephemera, small things that prompt regret…
Odd twinges in a limb cause them to fret,
while variously, on every night like this,
the rarest dreams are interrupted for a piss.

NET RESULT

There's a cool web of language winds us in
[Robert Graves, *Selected Poems*, 1957]

The self-perpetuating sphere our crowds are busy destroying
Should warn us life's no virtual realm whose language is inexact,
Where lies proliferate coolly and fiction can always trump fact.
Still, shit accumulates, is smoothly stirred, then smartly tossed about,
Hitting every fan. The clichés, arbitrary if annoying,
Click onward… New piles of outlandish crap, both crass and
    quick-drying,
Are swallowed by swelling masses. Joker, gossip or lonely lout,
Dull fanatic and airhead, strut axe-grinding stuff. Games are
    played out,
The Real World mirrored online—mainly greed, misplaced
    love, little tact.
Offence is taken, crimes denied: there's grudging, lame apology.
Thus entropy speeds up, the globe spinning its own necrology.

COLD SEASON

There's simply no escape from cliché or banality,
given this most mundane of subjects, whose totality
remains so disconcerting; few enough can face
examining the prospect with absolute composure.
Farewells near the terminus may ease the time of 'closure',
that academic and inadequate last word… The race,
however it is run, quite wrenchingly extends
to close and distant loves, as all acquaintances and friends,
partners and dear ones, disappear. It's just the human fate,

Though every fate may seem unjust to young or old,
pointless at worst, at best immortalised—stories retold
until the relics of emotion fade. They lie in wait,
these silent raids upon the once-articulate, cause pain
or bring a brief and raging joy. Thereafter nothing calms
the so-called soul. And if no phantoms tease the restless brain,
grief only gives one pause, invokes more unrelenting qualms,
seeks false insurance—*pace* outworn creeds. What dread,
what anguish burdens everyone, when musing on the dead!

NOTES

WRITERS AND THEIR WORKS
Writers and their Work [sic] was the title of a pamphlet series put out by the British Council from the 1940s on. Most of these introductory critical essays proved generally illuminating.

A CHANGING CITY GARDEN
Spanish leitmotiv as fragmented refrain, in Malcolm Lowry's great novel *Under the Volcano* (1947).

MOORE'S APPLES
Dr Moore, a veteran of the US Army Medical Corps in WW2, wrote two to five sonnets a day, having developed a 'compulsive addiction' to this form. His numerous collections included *M: One Thousand Autobiographical Sonnets*, 1938.

THE LATE READING
Variously quoted by Peter Reading in his later work.
Sunt aliquid manes; letum non omnia finit... (Ghosts in some form exist; death is not the end of everything). [Propertius Bk. IV.7]

THRENODY
Eheu fugaces...
[Horace Odes IV.14]
Opening lines addressed to a friend.

BATAILLE DU *MOI*
Georges Bataille (1897–1962). Influential French philosopher, critic and novelist. Author of the extraordinary erotic novel *Histoire de l'Oeil* (1st pub. 1928). *Histoire d'O* (1954) by 'Pauline Réage'/Dominique Aury was equally scandalous in its day. Aury's pseudonym Pauline Réage mischievously rings changes on the name of her lover Jean Paulhan, for whom the book was written to entertain and stimulate.